EXPLORING
AMERICA'S REGIONS

EXPLORING THE
MIDWEST

BY TAMMY GAGNE

CONTENT CONSULTANT
Pamela Riney-Kehrberg, PhD
Professor of History
Iowa State University

Core Library

An Imprint of Abdo Publishing
abdopublishing.com

Cover image: A boat travels along the Chicago River in
downtown Chicago, Illinois.

abdopublishing.com

Published by Abdo Publishing, a division of ABDO, PO Box 398166, Minneapolis, Minnesota 55439. Copyright © 2018 by Abdo Consulting Group, Inc. International copyrights reserved in all countries. No part of this book may be reproduced in any form without written permission from the publisher. Core Library™ is a trademark and logo of Abdo Publishing.

Printed in the United States of America, North Mankato, Minnesota
092017
012018

Cover Photo: Pawel Gaul/iStockphoto
Interior Photos: Pawel Gaul/iStockphoto, 1; K. Y. Phua/Shutterstock Images, 4–5, 43; Red Line Editorial, 6, 19; Kelly Humphrey/Brainerd Dispatch/AP Images, 10–11; Shutterstock Images, 16–17; NPS Photo, 20; iStockphoto, 22–23, 45; Debbie Center/Shutterstock Images, 25; Scott Sinklier/Newscom, 28–29; Sharon Laubscher/Wisconsin State Journal/AP Images, 31; Rebecca Cook/Reuters/Newscom, 33; Michael Matthews/Alamy, 34–35; Steve Skjold/Alamy, 39

Editor: Maddie Spalding
Imprint Designer: Maggie Villaume
Series Design Direction: Ryan Gale

Publisher's Cataloging-in-Publication Data

Names: Gagne, Tammy, author.
Title: Exploring the Midwest / by Tammy Gagne.
Description: Minneapolis, Minnesota : Abdo Publishing, 2018. | Series: Exploring America's regions | Includes online resources and index.
Identifiers: LCCN 2017946943 | ISBN 9781532113826 (lib.bdg.) | ISBN 9781532152702 (ebook)
Subjects: LCSH: Middle West--Juvenile literature. | Discovery and exploration--Juvenile literature. | Travel--Juvenile literature. | United States--Historical geography--Juvenile literature.
Classification: DDC 917.7--dc23
LC record available at https://lccn.loc.gov/2017946943

CONTENTS

CHAPTER ONE
America's Heartland **4**

CHAPTER TWO
History and Settlement **10**

CHAPTER THREE
Waterways and Landmarks **16**

CHAPTER FOUR
Animals and Plants **22**

CHAPTER FIVE
The Midwest's Economy **28**

CHAPTER SIX
Peoples and Cultures **34**

Fast Facts. 42

Stop and Think. 44

Glossary. 46

Online Resources 47

Learn More 47

Index 48

About the Author. 48

AMERICA'S HEARTLAND

The Midwest is known for its expansive lands. In some places, the windswept prairies look like they go on forever. The region has impressive waterways, too. Some of the largest rivers in the United States flow through here. The Midwest is also home to four of the five Great Lakes. These are the largest lakes in the country.

Because the region stretches across the central United States, it is often called America's Heartland. But geography is not the only reason for this nickname. The nickname

Kayakers explore Pictured Rocks National Lakeshore on Lake Superior.

THE MIDWEST REGION

Chapter One describes the landscapes of the Midwest. The map above shows the states, capitals, and some of the largest cities in the region. Does this map match your understanding of the region from the text? Why or why not?

also comes from the people's reputation for being friendly and down-to-earth.

The Midwest is made up of 12 states: Illinois, Indiana, Iowa, Kansas, Michigan, Minnesota, Missouri, Nebraska, North Dakota, Ohio, South Dakota, and Wisconsin. Much of the nation's corn, wheat, and livestock come from this region.

In the summer, hot weather is common in the Midwest. Temperatures can get up to 100 degrees Fahrenheit (38°C). The Midwest has no ocean breezes to cool the air. Winter is also harsh. Temperatures often fall below 0 degrees Fahrenheit (-18°C) in winter.

CITIES AND TOWNS

The Midwest's largest city is Chicago, Illinois. It is the third-largest city by population in the United States.

PERSPECTIVES
THE WINDY CITY

Many people call Chicago the "Windy City." This nickname is often linked to the strong breezes that blow through the area. But some people insist the nickname has another source. *New York Times* writer Jeff Zeleny explains: "If you had always assumed that Chicago earned its nickname as the Windy City from the chilly gusts coming off Lake Michigan, you would be wrong. The city is windy, according to most local legends, because of the hot air bellowing from politicians."

SMALL-TOWN ATTRACTIONS

The towns of Elk Horn and Kimballton are in Iowa. They have a combined population of approximately 950 people. But these tiny towns are the two largest rural Danish settlements in the United States. The only working Danish windmill in the country is in Elk Horn. It is one of the most popular tourist attractions in Iowa.

Other large cities in the Midwest include Columbus, Ohio; Detroit, Michigan; and Minneapolis, Minnesota. The Midwest also has many small cities and towns. Bayfield is a small town in Wisconsin. It is named after its harbor on Lake Superior. Just off the coast of this small town lie the Apostle Islands. People can kayak through caves or explore the islands' lighthouses. Mackinac Island in Michigan is a small but popular city to visit. On the island, cars are not allowed. People explore the area on horse-drawn carriages and bicycles. With so many places and landscapes to see, it's no wonder why millions of people choose to visit the Midwest each year.

STRAIGHT TO THE
SOURCE

New York Times journalist Curtis Sittenfeld and her husband moved to Saint Louis, Missouri, in 2007. Sittenfield was surprised by the kindness of complete strangers. She wrote:

> *It may take a year and a half to be invited to a dinner party, but the checkout clerk at the grocery store greets you as warmly as your grandmother . . . What I like best of all is that the size of St. Louis means we now run into people we know at the playground and the post office and the farmers' market. In several instances, we've developed friendships after we bumped into the same people in more than one setting. . . . Now I consider myself a St. Louis local.*

> Source: Curtis Sittenfeld. "Loving the Midwest." *New York Times*. New York Times, June 8, 2013. Web. Accessed May 12, 2017.

What's the Big Idea?
Read the primary source above carefully. What point is the author making about living in a small city? Make a list of two or three details that support this point.

HISTORY AND SETTLEMENT

The Midwest has an extensive history. Native American tribes lived in this area thousands of years before European explorers arrived. Native Americans from the Chippewa tribe lived in present-day Michigan, Wisconsin, Minnesota, and North Dakota. The Chippewa tribe is also often called the Ojibwe. The Lakota, Nakota, and Dakota tribes lived in the plains of the Midwest. The state of Illinois gets its name from the Illinois, or Illiniwek, tribe. The tribe lived in the Mississippi River Valley.

An Ojibwe dancer performs at a powwow in Onamia, Minnesota.

European settlers arrived in the region in the late 1600s. The French later fought with the British for land in the region. The Illinois fought alongside the French. This conflict was known as the French and Indian War (1754–1763). Other tribes in the area included the Shawnee and the Miami. The Shawnee lived in the Ohio Valley. They also were allies of the French. The Miami lived in what is now Indiana. They allied with the British. The British won the war. They took over land that belonged to the Illinois.

In the late 1700s, the US government tried to take over Native American lands in the Ohio Valley area. This led to the Northwest Indian War (1785–1795). The Shawnee, the Miami, and many other tribes in the area fought to keep their lands. But the Ohio Valley tribes were defeated by US troops. The Treaty of Greenville forced these tribes to surrender most of their lands to the US government in 1795.

HOMESTEADING

Many New Englanders moved to the Midwest in the mid-1800s. People came from other areas, too. The Homestead Act of 1862 drew many immigrants to the region. It promised free land for those willing to make the journey. Many homesteaders had no farming experience. But that did not stop them. Many German, Irish, and Scandinavian families settled in the Midwest. They hoped to earn a better living and make new lives for themselves.

HISTORIC EVENTS

The Midwest has often been a center

FORD'S MODEL T

The Midwest has been the site of impressive advances for the entire nation. One of the biggest was the introduction of the Model T automobile in Detroit, Michigan. Henry Ford's Ford Motor Company began using assembly lines to manufacture these cars in the early 1900s. By 1927, Ford had produced more than 15 million Model T cars. The Model T is now a thing of the past, but Ford remains one of the top US car companies.

THE KENT STATE SHOOTINGS

In 1970, many college students across the nation protested against the Vietnam War (1954–1975). On May 4, National Guardsmen arrived at a protest at Kent State University in Ohio. Mark Maedeker was a student there. He recalled, "I could see the side of the hill on the Commons where the [National Guardsmen] were. I started to walk outside. . . . I heard one initial shot and then a volley of shots. . . . I couldn't believe it when I found out they were using live ammunition." By the time the protest was over, the National Guardsmen had shot and killed four unarmed protestors.

for social change. In the 1950s, African Americans throughout the country were fighting for their civil rights. They were often not allowed the same opportunities as white Americans. An important court case helped change this. On May 17, 1954, the United States Supreme Court ruled on *Brown v. Board of Education*. Oliver Brown was an African American minister from Topeka, Kansas. He filed the lawsuit because the

Topeka school system denied his daughter admission to a white elementary school. The court decision deemed that separate schools for different races were not equal.

In 2008, the United States elected its first African-American president. Barack Obama gave his victory speech at Grant Park in Chicago. This Midwest location had been the site of violent protests against the Vietnam War during the 1968 presidential campaign. Now it was the site of a new era in American history.

FURTHER EVIDENCE

Chapter Two discusses Native American history in the Midwest. Identify one of the chapter's main points. What evidence is included to support this point? Take a look at the website below. Does the information on the website support an existing piece of evidence in the chapter? Or does it present new evidence?

NATIVE AMERICANS OF THE MIDWEST
abdocorelibrary.com/exploring-midwest

WATERWAYS AND LANDMARKS

Famous waterways and landmarks are found throughout the Midwest. Many landmarks make up the natural landscape. Others are man-made. Travelers and locals alike enjoy the region's sights.

One of the most important waterways is the Mississippi River. It stretches from Minnesota to the Gulf of Mexico in Louisiana. This river is the natural border for four midwestern states: Wisconsin, Iowa, Illinois, and Missouri.

The Gateway Arch in Saint Louis, Missouri, is a well-known landmark in the Midwest.

Four large lakes are located in the northern part of the Midwest. These are Lake Erie, Lake Huron, Lake Michigan, and Lake Superior. They are connected by rivers and straits. Together, they are part of the Great Lakes system. This is the largest freshwater system on the planet.

MAN-MADE SITES

Effigy Mounds National Monument is located in the Upper Mississippi River Valley. Prehistoric tribes created these earthen mounds as far back as 500 BCE. The mounds are burial sites. But how the tribes used them remains a mystery. The monument is made up of more than 200 mounds.

THE GREAT
LAKES

Many early settlers in the Midwest region chose to settle along the Great Lakes. The map below shows some of the towns and cities that were founded along the Great Lakes. What natural resources from the lakes might have made life easier for settlers?

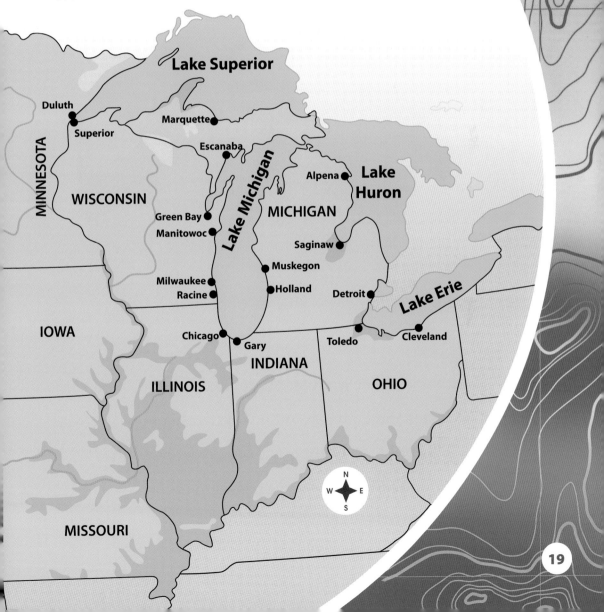

Mount Rushmore in the Black Hills of South Dakota honors four US presidents.

Some were sculpted in the shapes of animals, birds, or reptiles.

Another well-known man-made landmark in the Midwest is the Gateway Arch. This landmark is located in Saint Louis, Missouri. It honors Saint Louis as a starting point of westward expansion in the

United States. The arch stands 630 feet (192 m) tall at its highest point. Many people refer to the arch as the "Gateway to the West."

Each year, millions of people visit Mount Rushmore in South Dakota's Black Hills. Sculptor Gutzon Borglum carved the faces of four US presidents into the mountainside. The likenesses of George Washington, Thomas Jefferson, Theodore Roosevelt, and Abraham Lincoln are each approximately 60 feet (18 m) tall.

PERSPECTIVES

TALENTED ARTIST, TROUBLED MAN

Since Mount Rushmore's creation, historians have discovered that Gutzon Borglum was not an upstanding person. Author John Taliaferro wrote a book about Mount Rushmore called *Great White Fathers*. In it, he shared his research about Borglum's connection with the Ku Klux Klan. This hate group has a long history of violence against non-white people in the United States. Many people find this connection especially troubling in light of Mount Rushmore's location. The Black Hills are sacred to the Lakota and many other Native American tribes.

ANIMALS AND PLANTS

The Midwest is home to a variety of animals and plants. Some are native to the area. Others were brought from different states or countries. Some of these introduced species have become abundant in the Midwest.

WILDLIFE IN THE MIDWEST

As many as 30 million bison once roamed throughout North America. Native Americans relied on these animals to make food, clothing, and tools. But European settlers later overhunted bison. The bison

Bison graze on prairie grass in Custer State Park, South Dakota.

THE GRAY WOLF'S ENDANGERED STATUS

Gray wolves were once endangered in the Midwest. Populations have increased in recent years. Some people think it is time to remove the animal from the Endangered Species list. In 2017, US representative Collin Peterson wrote a letter to congressional leaders. He said: "Cows and their calves can easily be worth several thousand dollars, so each instance of a wolf attack has devastating economic impacts on ranchers and their families. Currently, ranchers and farmers have no legal actions available to deal with gray wolf attacks because these predators are federally protected." But many people worry that without protections, gray wolves will become threatened again.

population declined. Today, approximately 500,000 bison live on preserves and ranches. They have remained a cultural symbol of the Great Plains. The Great Plains are expansive prairie lands west of the Mississippi River.

While bison graze on the midwestern prairie, eagles fly above it. In the winter, golden eagles migrate south from Canada or Alaska. They settle in southeastern Minnesota, western Wisconsin, and

Bald eagles make their homes in tall trees.

northeastern Iowa. Bald eagles also live throughout the Midwest. They hunt for fish in lakes and rivers.

Prairie dogs are also common in the Midwest. These small mammals are related to squirrels. They play an important role in midwestern ecosystems. They feed on plants and small grasses. They serve as prey for predators, such as golden eagles. Like bison, prairie dogs once existed in much greater numbers in this region. But many ranchers saw the species as a pest and killed them. Today, prairie dogs are protected in many of the region's state and national parks.

PLANTS OF THE MIDWEST

The plants in the Midwest are as diverse as the states that make up the region. Some of the plants and trees can be found in other parts of the country. But some plant species are unique to the Midwest. The Midwest Manchurian crabapple tree grows throughout all midwestern states. It can also be found in Montana, Wyoming, and Colorado.

THE MIDWEST'S TOP CROP

Most of the corn produced in the United States is grown in the Midwest. Besides being eaten as food, corn is used to make a variety of products. It is used to make corn flour, cornmeal, and grits. Corn crops also help feed the nation's livestock. Corn can even be turned into a fuel called ethanol.

This species is native to northeast Asia. But it thrives in the Midwest because it can survive in cold weather. It is also resistant to many diseases that affect other trees.

One of the most common flowers in the Midwest is the black-eyed Susan. It can survive harsh midwestern winters. Black-eyed Susans are related to sunflowers. Sunflowers are also common in the Midwest. Kansas is nicknamed "the Sunflower State." Many sunflowers grow wild across Kansas's prairies.

EXPLORE ONLINE

Chapter Four talks about animals that live in the Midwest. The website below focuses on prairie dogs. How is the information from the website the same as the information in Chapter Four? What new information did you learn from the website?

ABOUT PRAIRIE DOGS

abdocorelibrary.com/exploring-midwest

THE MIDWEST'S ECONOMY

Farming and manufacturing are the backbone of the midwestern economy. The region's soil and climate make it ideal for growing a variety of crops. And the Midwest's large, open spaces often create perfect spots for large companies to build factories.

FARMING

Much of the Midwest is called the Corn Belt due to its most important crop. Western Indiana, Illinois, Iowa, Missouri, eastern Nebraska, and eastern Kansas all make up this area. Iowa grows more corn than

A farmer uses a tractor to harvest corn in rural Iowa.

DO ONE THING RIGHT

Some small farms in the Midwest are struggling. They cannot afford all of the modern machinery that makes larger farms successful. Animal scientist and activist Dr. Temple Grandin advises ranchers on how to survive in this competitive industry. In an interview with the National Young Farmers Coalition, she said: "One of the things the small farmer needs to do is have a niche that the big companies don't fill. . . . Find a specialized niche—natural, organic, grassfed, etc.— and develop the market. Sell locally. Sell to a large population center. That can make a real good living."

any other state. Approximately 20 percent of all corn in the United States is grown in Iowa.

The top crop in Kansas is wheat. Kansas is the top wheat-growing state. Approximately one-third of farmers in Kansas grow wheat. Half of the wheat the state grows is kept in the United States. The other half is exported to other parts of the world. The wheat is

A Wisconsin dairy farmer tends to her cows.

then made into many different products, such as bread or cereal.

Dairy farming is another major industry in the Midwest. Dairy farmers raise cows for their milk. More than 9,000 dairy herds are located in Wisconsin. Wisconsin is often nicknamed "America's Dairyland." It leads the country in cheese production. The state makes more than 2.5 billion pounds (1.1 billion kg) of cheese each year.

MANUFACTURING

Michigan manufactures more automobiles than any other state in the country. For this reason, Detroit is often called "Motor City." Detroit is home to Ford

Workers build cars at a Ford assembly plant in Flat Rock, Michigan.

Motor Company, General Motors, and Fiat Chrysler. These companies make up 3 percent of the nation's economy. They provide more manufacturing jobs than any other industry.

Other manufacturing companies in the Midwest build airplanes. Boeing is a midwestern-based company that makes commercial and military aircraft. It has had manufacturing facilities in Saint Louis for more than 80 years. Boeing finished building a large Saint Louis production facility in October 2016. It is expected to add approximately 700 jobs to the area in the next few years. Boeing's headquarters are located in Chicago.

PEOPLES AND CULTURES

Some influential people have come from the Midwest. President Abraham Lincoln grew up in Indiana and Illinois. Writer F. Scott Fitzgerald hailed from Saint Paul, Minnesota. But the people who perhaps best represent the spirit of the modern Midwest are the ones living there today.

NATIVE AMERICAN COMMUNITIES

The US government forced many Native Americans in the Midwest to leave their homes during the 1800s. Some of these tribes now live in different parts of the country. The Shawnee

Dancers perform at the Oglala Lakota Nation Powwow on Pine Ridge Indian Reservation in South Dakota.

reservation is in Oklahoma. Many descendants of the Illinois tribe also now live in Oklahoma. They joined the Peoria tribe.

Many tribal members in the Midwest work to preserve their cultures and traditions. People belonging to the Illinois and Miami tribes mainly speak English now. But earlier generations spoke the Miami-Illinois language. Some older tribal members still know this language. They continue to pass down this knowledge to later generations.

Miami University in Oxford, Ohio, was named after the tribe of the same name. The school has a close relationship with tribal leaders still living in the area. The school offers educational opportunities for students interested in learning about the history, culture, and issues the tribe faces in the present era.

Other Native American communities within the Midwest include the Chippewa, Potawatomi, Lakota, Nakota, and Dakota. Today, the Chippewa live mainly in

Minnesota, Wisconsin, and Michigan. The Potawatomi live mainly in the Great Lakes area. Lakota, Dakota, and Nakota Native Americans live mainly in North and South Dakota.

GERMAN CULTURE

In many parts of the Midwest, people of German descent make up much of the population. German people immigrated to the Midwest in large numbers in the mid-1800s. Many were escaping famine and economic hardships in Germany. They were also fleeing political conflicts.

People interested in learning more about German-American culture can visit a variety of places in the Midwest. One such

GOING FISHING

Fishing is often a year-round activity in the Midwest. Many midwesterners go ice fishing in the winter. Fishing is both a popular sport and a source of food. After people catch fish, they often hold fish fries. These are large social gatherings where people enjoy a tasty meal and the company of others.

place is the Germanic-American Institute in Saint Paul, Minnesota. This institute educates the public about German-American culture. The German American Heritage Center & Museum in Davenport, Iowa, offers classes and exhibits. Folklore Village in Dodgeville, Wisconsin, holds German concerts and other festivities.

RECENT IMMIGRANTS

Many recent immigrants to the United States live in the Midwest region. Large waves of refugees from Southeast Asia arrived in the United

Hmong dancers perform at the Dragon Festival in Saint Paul, Minnesota.

States beginning in the 1970s. Many of them belonged to the Hmong ethnic group. They had been driven out of several Asian countries during and after the Vietnam War. Approximately half of the Hmong people in the United States today live in Midwest. Most of them settled in Michigan, Minnesota, and Wisconsin. Each year, the city of Saint Paul, Minnesota, hosts the Dragon Festival. This festival celebrates the state's Asian communities.

Large populations of other immigrant groups have also settled in the Midwest. Minnesota has more Somali immigrants than any other US state. Chicago has the second-largest Mexican immigrant population of any US city. Mexican and Latin American immigrants also make up a large part of other areas in the Midwest. Almost half of the people who work on Wisconsin's dairy farms are from Mexico.

The Midwest is home to a variety of people who have helped make the region what it is today. With its food on tables across the nation, the Midwest has also become a powerful player in the national economy. This region is sure to play a significant role in the future of the United States.

STRAIGHT TO THE
SOURCE

Amy Thielen is a chef who hosts a Food Network show called *The Heartland Table*. This show is filmed in a cabin near Park Rapids, Minnesota. In a 2014 interview, Thielen explained how midwestern food and culture differs from other parts of the country:

> To me, the big difference in dining between New York City and the Midwest is informality. Things are more relaxed here in the Midwest, and that's not a bad thing. Whether in restaurants or [at] home entertaining, you see more casual entertaining. . . . I actually don't think you can distill the Midwest into one food culture; it's such a mixture of different regional influences. You have Scandinavian influences, German influences . . . Collective taste memory is the common thread, and it's constantly evolving.

> Source: Vanessa Druckman. "Interview: Amy Thielen of Food Network's *The Heartland Table*." *Chefdruck* (blog). Vanessa Druckman, March 10, 2014. Web. Accessed June 10, 2017.

Back It Up
The author of this passage is using evidence to support a point. Write a paragraph describing the point the author is making. Then write down two or three pieces of evidence the author uses to make the point.

FAST FACTS

- Total Area: 821,872 square miles (2.1 million sq km)

- Population: Approximately 68 million people

- Largest City: Chicago, Illinois

- Largest State by Population: Illinois

- Smallest State by Population: North Dakota

- Largest State by Land Size: Kansas

- Smallest State by Land Size: Indiana

- Highest Point: Black Elk Peak in South Dakota, 7,242 feet (2,207 m) above sea level

- Lowest Point: Saint Francis River in Missouri, 230 feet (70 m) above sea level

- Rivers: The two longest rivers in the United States, the Mississippi River and the Missouri River, flow through the Midwest.

- Lakes: All four of the Great Lakes in the Midwest border the state of Michigan.

- Tornadoes: A large area in the Midwest is known as Tornado Alley because tornadoes are more common in this part of the country. This area includes parts of South Dakota, Nebraska, and Kansas.

STOP AND
THINK

Tell the Tale

Chapter One of this book discusses the states that make up the Midwest. Imagine that you are planning a weeklong road trip to this region. Which states would you want to visit first? Which attractions would interest you most? Write 200 words about all the things you would want to do and see in this part of the Midwest.

Dig Deeper

After reading this book, what questions do you still have about the Midwest? With an adult's help, find a few reliable sources that will help you answer these questions. Write a paragraph about what you learned.

Say What?

Reading a book about a region of the United States can mean learning a lot of new vocabulary. Find five words in this book that you had not seen before. Use a dictionary to find out what they mean. Then write the meanings in your own words, and use each word in a new sentence.

You Are There

Chapter Three talks about several popular landmarks in the Midwest. Imagine you have visited one of these attractions. Write a letter home telling your family and friends about your experience. Be sure to add plenty of details.

GLOSSARY

ambience
a feeling or mood related to a particular place

civil rights
citizens' rights to political and social equality

culture
the customs, beliefs, and traditions held by a group of people

ecosystem
all living and nonliving things in a particular environment

ethanol
an alcohol-based fuel made from grains such as corn

ethnic
associated with a specific nation or culture

famine
a widespread shortage of food

homesteading
the exchange of public land to private owners for their willingness to work on and develop it

niche
relating to products or services that appeal to a small group of people

reservation
an area of land set aside by the federal government for use by a Native American tribe

ONLINE
RESOURCES

To learn more about the midwestern region of the United States, visit our free resource websites below.

Visit **abdocorelibrary.com** for free Common Core resources for teachers and students, including vetted activities, multimedia, and booklinks, for deeper subject comprehension.

Visit **abdobooklinks.com** for free additional online weblinks for further learning. These links are routinely monitored and updated to provide the most current information available.

LEARN
MORE

Bekkering, Annalise. *Great Lakes*. New York: AV2 by Weigl, 2013.

Wiseman, Blaine. *The People of the Midwest*. New York: AV2 by Weigl, 2014.

INDEX

bison, 23–24
Black Hills, 21
Borglum, Gutzon, 21
Brown v. Board of Education, 14–15

Chippewa Native Americans, 11, 36–37
climate, 7

Dakota Native Americans, 11, 36–37

eagles, 24–25, 26
Effigy Mounds National Monument, 18, 20

farming industry, 26, 29–30, 32

French and Indian War, 12

Gateway Arch, 20–21
Great Lakes, 5, 18–19, 37
Great Plains, 24

Illinois Native Americans, 11–12, 36
immigrants, 13, 37–40

Lakota Native Americans, 11, 21, 36–37
Lincoln, Abraham, 21, 35

manufacturing industry, 13, 32–33
Miami Native Americans, 12, 36

Mississippi River, 17
Mount Rushmore, 21

Nakota Native Americans, 11, 36–37
Northwest Indian War, 12

plants, 26–27
Potawatomi Native Americans, 36–37
prairie dogs, 25–27

Shawnee Native Americans, 12, 35–36

Vietnam War, 14, 15, 39

About the Author

Tammy Gagne has authored dozens of books for both adults and children. She has written about culture, geography, and nature conservation. She lives in northern New England with her husband, son, and pets.